THIS MIRACULOUS TURNING

This
Miraculous
Turning

JOSEPH MILLS

Press 53
Winston-Salem

Press 53, LLC
PO Box 30314
Winston-Salem, NC 27130

First Edition

Cover design by Kevin Morgan Watson

Cover art, "Untitled," Copyright © 2014
by Kenneth Frazelle, used by permission of the artist.

Author photo by Danielle Tarmey

Printed on acid-free paper
ISBN 978-1-941209-09-7

To Noelle and Benjamin,
who teach me every day

Acknowledgments

The author wishes to thank the following publications where these poems (or earlier versions of them) first appeared.

After Hours: "What We Haven't Read"
Charlotte View: "The End," "What We Still May Have Left"
Cobalt Review: "Death and My Daughter: A Timeline," "For Unknown Reasons"
Common-Place: A Journal of Early American Life: "Fragments of Education," "Passivity," "Singing in God's Acre"
Connotations Press: "The Girl in the Second-Story Window," "Savings," "We've Had This Conversation Before"
The Dead Mule School of Southern Literature: "Azaleas," "Trespass" (as "Barking"), "We Were Only Going to Stay a Year or Two"
Germ Magazine: "Birth Poems," "Here," "Questions"
Gingerbread House: "Street Life, or When My Kids and I Go Out" (as "When We Walk Out the Door My Kids Make Me a Kind of Badass")
The Helix: "Valentine's Day"
I-70 Review: "Ascension"
Iodine Poetry Review: "Catch," "The Question"
The Lake: "Landscaping," "So Spring Is Icumen In"
Main Street Rag: "Market," "The Music of the Land"
One: "What Parents Eat"
The Penmen Review: "The Next Door Neighbor," "The Unfinished Work"
Pinesong: "The Education Process"
Provo Canyon Review: "The Last Speakers of the Language," "The Systematic Treatment of Magnitude"
Sliver of Stone: "Branded"
storySouth: "Simple Architecture"
Stirring: "Bound," "Carnal Knowledge," "The Color Wheel,"
Stymie: A Journal of Sport and Literature: "Factory Kids"
The Tau: "Role Models"
The Tower Journal: "Art Life," "At the Book Festival My Daughter and I Walk Away from the Truth," "The Problem with Grades," "Relativity," "Wash"
Upstart: A Journal of Renaissance Literature: "Enter Bottom"
What Matters: "My Daughter Continues To Be Annoyed By George Washington"
The Wild Goose Review: "Digging to China," "Swimming Lessons"

This Miraculous Turning

I. THE EDUCATION PROCESS

II. WALKING MY CHILDREN THROUGH GRAVEYARDS

III. THE LAST SPEAKERS OF A LANGUAGE

I.

THE EDUCATION PROCESS

The Education Process

After surveying the school's carnival booths,
I lead my three-year-old son to "Dino-Dig,"
a wading pool filled with Styrofoam peanuts
where you plunge in your hands and trawl
for prizes, like a toy Triceratops or Stegosaurus.
But, he doesn't understand how to do this.
He wants to climb in, then pretends to wash,
then he simply splashes the pieces around.
"Look," I say, "Like this." I push into the foam
and bring up a Brontosaurus and Brachiosaurus.
Perhaps it's unreasonable, even cruel, to ask him
to play archaeologist since he can't find his pants
when he's standing on them, but others help
by pushing figures close. Finally, he grasps one.

Before anyone can cheer, he tosses it back.
The boys in line complain, so I scoop out
a Pterodactyl and pull him away. He heads
for the bouncy slide, the biggest rip-off there,
especially since free slides are across the street.
I suggest the ring toss where he'll get a prize,
but he is adamant. I give him a couple tickets,
then more tickets, and finally, all of them,
and I watch as he spends an entire afternoon
falling towards the earth, giggling, not caring
that when it's time to go, he's empty-handed,
except for the blue dinosaur he doesn't want,
the one in my pocket jabbing me with its beak
as if trying to convince me I should let it go.

Swimming Lessons

My wife and I are swimmers from families
of swimmers, so we expected our daughter
would be a swimmer, and we're surprised
that she refuses to put her head underwater.
If even a drop touches her face, she cries out
and gropes for a towel. Nothing we try works,
so we sign her up for lessons with Mrs. White,
who soon has her swimming lengths of the pool.
I watch and wonder what I could have learned
from my parents had they not been my parents.
Afterwards, my daughter runs up, laughing,
"Did you see me, Daddy?" and I swing her high,
pat her face dry with my tie as the teacher says,
smiling, "She has a very good black...Her black...

I'm sorry... Her BACKstroke will be good."
She looks embarrassed, and I understand.
A white parent and a black child can knock
the most well-meaning people off balance.
Since Mrs. White is black, I want to laugh,
instead I say, "That's good." My daughter
senses something has surfaced unexpectedly
then submerged, just as she feels something
is odd when people look past me to locate
her parents or ask, "Is she yours?" Someday
she'll understand more about the currents
around us and why we insisted she learn
to swim. Someday, she may even realize
how clenched we are each time she goes in.

The Systematic Treatment of Magnitude

When our son reads a church sign as "Jesus Christ Plus,"
then asks, "Plus what?" we realize we've been neglecting
his religious instruction, but this doesn't seem the time,
as we eat ice cream, to explain the cross and crucifixion.

Besides, maybe he's right, and it's Jesus Christ and More.
Or a New and Improved Church for the Plus-Size Christian.
Now 50% wider pews! Super-sized wafers! Cupholders!
And, after all, wouldn't many agree Christ adds to one's life?

Aren't most religions a type of mathematics? The equals
of Tao, the subtractions of Buddhism, the five Islamic pillars,
the gematria of Judaism, the postulating for variables, X—
this life—and Y—this world—and ways to solve for each.

"I know a bunch of pluses," my son says, and as he recites
2+2=4, 3+3=6, 4+4=8, I hear the catechism of my youth.
He walks on, confident in his doctrine, as I uneasily consider
what's in my hands and try to calculate how long it may last.

Wash

As the man washes the neighbor's car,
he keeps glancing at our house
and the children riding bikes
on the sidewalk. Finally he walks over
to where I'm painting shingles
and asks, "Where are they from?"
When I say, "We live here," he says,
"But where did you adopt them from?"
He expects to hear Haiti or Africa,
and when I say, "They were born here,"
he recoils like I've struck him.

After a moment, he reaches out
to shake my hand. I show him
that mine is smeared with paint,
but he grasps it anyway,
his skin damp and soap-slick.
"What church do you go to?" he asks.
When I say we don't, he shakes his head.
"At my church we have a lot of couples
who want to adopt babies from China.
Never here. Never ours." I don't know
what to say to this. I don't say anything.
"Thank you," he says. "God bless you."
I don't say anything to this either.
He smiles at the children pedaling past,
who look at him curiously, then he crosses
the street. The neighbor inspects the car,
and, unsatisfied, makes him wash it again.

Digging to China

We easily stripped away
the grass and a sheet of dirt
before hitting rock
that snapped off the tip
of the garden spade.

We bent the blades
of snow shovels against it,
buckled and broke knives,
shattered the handles
of several screwdrivers
by hitting them with mallets.
We used hammers and sledges
and a crowbar to little effect.

When we asked an older sister
to get us firecrackers, M-80s,
some kind of explosives,
she walked behind the garage,
surveyed the shallow basin
we had gouged in the yard,
and said, *You can't get there
like that.* Her tone said
we were idiots, but I heard,
like that.
                    Like

                              That.

It was possible.
You could get there.
Somehow.

First Skating Party

Dozens of kids circle
the worn wooden floor
on old rental skates,
and none of them wear
helmets or pads,
so when they collide
or fall or stop themselves
by the simple technique
of steering straight
into the cinder-block barrier,
you can feel the pain
of the parents
who watch from booths
by the concession stand;
they know their children
have bones of balsa
and skin that tears
as easily as a napkin,
but they can do nothing
except yell, *Be Careful!*
and make hand gestures
to slow down
                    —Slow Down!—
as the ones they love
strobe past them
faster and faster
just beyond their reach.

The Problem with Grades

She can barely stand on her skates,
her ankles bending like plastic rulers,
yet somehow she has ended up
in the middle of the rink, stranded
in that empty island of space.
She seems close to tears, but determined
not to cry. No one notices. No one stops.
They circle past, again and again,
and then one boy, about her size,
heads towards her like someone
dogpaddling into deep water.
When he reaches her, they clasp hands
and try to work out how to move together,
a combination of chop-stepping, coasting
and holding one another upright.
They cut straight across the lane,
as skaters swerve around them,
and eventually reach the safety
of the cinder-block wall. There,
she moors herself, and he moves away
without a glance, then, after a moment,
she pushes herself back out onto the rink.

The Color Wheel

My daughter says, "Daddy, Brandon called me black,
and when I said I was milk chocolate, he said, 'No,
you're black.'" She's puzzled by the exchange, and
when I explain, "People will call you black and me
white," she finds this difficult to believe. She learned
colors ages ago, in daycare, including ranges of hues.
To say she's black when she's actually cocoa brown
makes no sense. It's oddly crude like something
a baby would do. And, my skin looks nothing like
the paper in our printer or the kitchen appliances.
She doesn't understand this willful misapplication
of words. To her, it seems almost indistinguishable
from lying, and there was something else, something
in his tone, an insistence, an unexpected vehemence.

Her vision changes now that she knows she's black;
she sees how black goes second in chess, and how
the behavior stick at school gets moved from green
to red to black. She sees the way people are seen,
and moves a little farther away when we walk
to the car. She wants to know if it would be okay
if I didn't come to school for lunches anymore.
Then one day, I hear her talking about a boy
in her class, and to make it clear who she means,
since two of them have the same name, she says,
"You know, the black one." And there it is,
the education process, the turning of the wheel
from the complex colors she knows each of us to be
to the blunt ones she has learned we insist on using.

Valentine's Day

On the ride home from school,
the kids examine their cards
and discuss the weaponry
of love. Cupid's bow and arrows
seem flimsy. Wouldn't a crossbow
be better? Or a rifle?
One boy suggests a bazooka,
and his best friend agrees.
A diapered baby with a bazooka
blowing up everything in sight
would be totally awesome.
The girls wait for the barrage
of laughter to subside,
then one says, "That's stupid.
You don't know anything
about love." For a moment,
there is shocked silence,
then the wounded boy,
who for several weeks
has been casually careful to sit
where he can kick the girl's seat,
counters, "Oh yeah?
Even if I had the biggest gun
in the whole entire world
I wouldn't shoot you.
Not even once."

Enter Romeo. Enter Juliet.

The fifth grade performs *Romeo and Juliet* each May,
and the whole school attends, so the students see
this boy-girl tale, this double suicide, in kindergarten
then again and again and again and again and again.
No one expects a play about Elmo or Dora the Explorer,
(although at least she would be a strong girl with the sense
not to get overwrought about a muppet). But it is odd,
this annual insistence on a world of such violence.
Perhaps the problem is the season. This isn't a tale
to tell in spring—it is no love story—but rather one
for October. Acknowledge the play as the nightmare
it is, how it casts our children as Juliets and Romeos,
how it forces us to watch as they kill themselves
vainly, and then how we are expected to applaud.

Role Models

While the girls are asleep
or locked in their rooms,
the boys have been cast out.

A few may be charming,
but the stories make clear
most will be monstrous:
kidnappers, wolves,
giants, and trolls.
If they rule, it will be badly.
At best, they will be inept,
unable to protect their families;
more often they'll be tyrants
to be overthrown and destroyed.
Sometimes they will simply
disappear from the story,
and no one will notice.

These tales tell possible futures
with the blunt indifference
of a burnt-out guidance counselor.
No wonder some decide
they might as well
get an early start
on acting big and bad,
becoming at least someone
people talk about.

Turning

My friend's kid runs the sideline, gets a pass,
turns, and scores with a kick to the near post.

It's how the play should go, but at this age
rarely does. My son sprints to him, arms up.

They high five and celebrate a moment,
then turn to jog back to their positions.

Last year, they would have hopped around madly,
twirled, fallen backwards, and rolled in the grass.

This season, they are serious. No more
skipping. No more acting sweetly goofy.

Now, they turn towards one another rather
than towards us. No more checking that we've seen.

But we have. We know the score, and what's lost
as they try to turn themselves into men.

Factory Kids

Coach grabbed my face guard,
yanked me towards him
like I was a dog,
yelled, *Goddamnit,*
I want you
to make him hurt.
Do you understand me?

I did. We all did.
We knew even then, as boys
being taught, we thought,
how to be men,
what it meant to hurt
and how much worse it was
to be made to hurt.

Carnal Knowledge

When I asked Tony what fucking was,
he took me out back and told me about women,
how they have three holes in their sides,
which made me imagine some combination
of electrical outlet and the wounds of Christ,
(an idea solidified later when I heard
how women bled and how dangerous it was
to put anything in there), and he explained
how a woman was a woman and a man
was a man and that women wanted men
to be men and that a man needed a woman
who was a woman, and I felt he was sharing
secrets of adulthood, but after hearing them,
I still didn't understand what fucking was;
then one night Greg and I knocked on his door
and Tony walked up, stood behind the screen,
and pointed a twelve-gauge straight at us,
saying, "Don't fuck with me," and we laughed
until he broke the barrel and popped shells out,
and something inside me wrenched around
and I realized even people you think you know
behave differently, dangerously, in the dark.

Enter Bottom

As we drank Budweiser on the hood
of Gary's Oldsmobile Cutlass,
we looked at the lights on the lake
and talked about what we might do—
ask out Cathy or Cindy or Nancy,
become lawyers, doctors,
hell, maybe even President,
tell off that son-of-a-bitch
of an assistant manager,
of a teacher, of a coach—

and, right then, we believed
we could. We could
leave the town, somehow,
and be transformed.
We had heard stories
where it had happened,
tales of someone's sibling
going away and becoming
the type of person
seen in magazine ads.

As the night went on,
we would get louder,
not knowing or caring
if anyone heard us,
our voices a melody
of yearning and desperation
fragmenting against the trees.

We just wanted something
to do, some kind of role,
any of them, all of them,
ones that meant something
if only to asses like us.

Art Life

On a family walk, I notice a For Sale sign,
and, as I read the listing, the daughter notices
a small statue of David in the yard. She asks,
"Why is that guy naked?" which makes the son
stop bouncing his soccer ball, stare, then yell,
"I can see his wiener!" I say, "That's David,
who fought Goliath. It's a famous art work."
They scrutinize the sculpture and both agree
it would be stupid to fight naked like that
although the slingshot would be cool to have.
The daughter asks, "What's that design for
above his penis?" I explain it's pubic hair,
and she's surprised. The doctor gave her
a brochure on puberty, and she's read it
several times, but none of its graphics
look anything like that. She leans on the fence
to get a better view. I note hair can be hard
for artists to do, and the son announces,
"I have tons of pubic hair. Tons and tons."
"No, you don't," I say, "You will someday,
but your sister will be getting hers first."
He mutters, "No fair," turning away,
and I'm relieved at this decline in interest.
Lately his mother and I have been trying
to get him to stop taking off his pants,
so I had been afraid of this counter-example.
His sister continues to consider the statue.
Finally she asks, "Daddy, do you want
to buy this house?" When I say, "No,"
she seems relieved. "Do you?" I ask.
She shakes her head. "Who wants to live
with a naked guy outside all the time?"

Street Life, or When My Kids and I Go Out

Some see me as the Erl King,
spiriting children away, and some
as a kind of saint, rescuing them
from God knows what sort of life.
Many feel sorry I had to settle
for second-hand kids (otherwise,
I would have had ones of my own);
while others admire me as a picker
who has sorted through junked lives
and recognized pieces of value.
I'm naïve, a colonialist, an idealist,
a social worker, a buyer of children,
capitalist, slaver, Rumplestiltskin.

The balding middle-aged white man
isn't particularly noteworthy until
he's next to young black children.
Have them hold his hand as they walk,
and suddenly there's a soundtrack,
bass lines, the whistling of a Western,
a heavenly choir. And there are tremors,
hinting at an avalanche of images
and ideas triggered by their being
who they are, together, going for milk.

The Next Door Neighbor

As we unload the truck, she yells
from a metal chair on her porch,
I've seen 'em come and seen 'em go,
and it's clear she expects to do both
with us. Later, at the housewarming,
she says she learned to smoke upstairs
in our bathroom sixty years ago,
that the neighborhood has changed,
and things aren't the same,
that she used to be a dance teacher
but she retired at the right time
since her students had all started
to listen to that nigger music.
She says it'd be nice to have someone
clean her gutters, and she looks at me.
I agree, yes, that certainly would be nice.

When we adopt our daughter, she says
the woman down the street asked her
why we couldn't get a white baby,
but she thinks we've done a good thing,
that the baby is lucky, and we'll be blessed,
and I want to say, Fuck you,
you racist old bat. Aren't you afraid
what you'll hear from our house?
I want to say we're not blessed
or "good people." But what I say is,
We're the ones who are lucky.
I say, *I hope the late-night crying
isn't too loud.* I say, *It looks like rain.*

And one day we realize our daughter
is gone. She's not in the house or yard
and we find her on the neighbor's porch,
chatting away. *She's good company,*
the woman says, and, from then on,
each time our child goes outside,

the woman yells from her chair,
Here comes Miss America!
She starts buying gifts at Food Lion,
plastic toys and discounted candy
that she brings over after church.
She tells us, *You need to get that girl
brothers and sisters. It's a terrible thing
to grow old alone. A terrible thing.*

After her cat dies, she finally agrees
to move into a home and it's not long
after that the operations start.
Once, she gets someone to drive her
by the house, but she's too weak
to get out of the car. She tells us
they probably mean well enough
at the new place, *but I miss my porch.
I miss that beautiful girl of yours.
It's not the same. Things aren't the same.*

At the Book Festival My Daughter and I Turn Away from the Truth

When I see the guy in a Confederate uniform
standing by a stack of books announcing,
The Truth About Slavery, I look around for
my daughter, and I'm relieved to find her
at a table with balloons and a candy bowl.

I used to be more interested in truth,
but now when someone starts to explain
The Truth About Women, Men, Blacks,
Whites, The President, America, God,
I sidle away. This author may be innocuous,

even friendly. He might smile at my child,
something that happens frequently enough
to suggest there's some fundamental belief
nothing shows you're not racist like smiling
at a black kid. He might even be right about

whatever he's written, but my daughter and I
decide to leave the festival, turning our backs
on the truth to search for ice cream, a park,
a playground with swings, some kind of pleasure
and beauty we can share in our time together.

The Unfinished Work

For every Southern boy fourteen years old, not once but whenever he wants it, there is the instant when it's still not yet two o'clock on that July afternoon in 1863…
—William Faulkner, *Intruders in the Dust*

I had been to Gettysburg twice before,
with my brother, and we had searched
for monuments to our native Indiana,
trying to imagine ourselves back then,
stationed in some rifle pit or trench,
pointing a weapon at the line of gray
doomed men stepping from the woods.
We understood we would have been
scared and homesick, but also resolute,
grimly determined to make America
into America, the nation of destiny,
winner of world wars, the United States
of John Wayne and John Ford.

This time I'm with my European wife
and our two children, who want to find
the monuments for their home state,
North Carolina, ones on the other side
of the field, a place I've never gone,
and as we look at maps and displays
of troop movements, my son asks,
"Daddy, where would I have been?"
His older sister looks at me, then him.
She has long understood their skin
means a different place in these stories.
It wouldn't have been as simple for them
as marching off to one side or the other.
But, although my son knows he's brown,
he doesn't yet understand he's "black,"
and I wonder what to say. I know
stories of soldiers who looked like him,
and those of slaves. Which ones to tell
right now? Which do my children need?
Which will harm? Which will help?
Which will show not what their places
might have been, but what they can be?

What my son does understand already,
looking from the ridge to the woods,
is what it would mean to have to walk
all the way across this field when people
on the other side have cannons and guns.
"It wouldn't make any sense to do that,"
he says. "That would just be dumb."

We begin to go past the monuments
without reading them, content
to simply be walking in the sun.
Although the cemetery is nearby,
and we think we should visit it,
the kids have seen a McDonalds
at the edge of the battlefield, and
it's sparked a determined campaign
to get a treat before dinner, so
we go back to the van, a Toyota,
a brand my mother calls "Jap junk,"
and thinks is shameful we own
because she has "friends who fought
in Vietnam." And, as we leave the lot,
we argue about whose turn it is
to pick music and how we should go
to wherever it is we're going next.
Nothing is as clear as the markers,
maps, and books make it seem,
particularly the entangled desires
of family. Later, each of us might
make up stories about these days,
trying, in retrospect, to make sense
of what we did and why, our lives
together, the unfinished work.

In the Gettysburg Cyclorama
Depicting Pickett's Charge

my daughter looks at the scenes
as paintings, trying to figure out
the techniques and find the seams
between canvases, and my son sees

the action as a movie or TV series,
an exciting adventure story,
although the wounded horses
make him uneasy, and my wife stands

motionless, silently weeping,
holding the hands of our children,
who are not much younger than those
dying around us, and I am fighting

the claustrophobia of being enclosed
by this bowl of history and wondering
where the exit is and if one may be how
my daughter looks at the scenes

What Parents Eat

As my son swings
and says *Daddy*
> *look at me.*

> *I'm magic!*

a boy is shot for being
in an unfamiliar neighborhood

a boy is shot for asking
for help

> a boy is shot
for walking in the backyard
of a house his father just bought

a boy is shot for being
a boy

> like my son

curving into the sky
then falling towards earth

and again
> I must speak
with my mouth full

of fear
> the daily bread
I will eat
until one of us dies

and I try to swallow
> and I say

Yes, you are.
> *Yes, you are.*

II.

WALKING MY CHILDREN
THROUGH GRAVEYARDS

or

On Raising Kids near Old Salem, North Carolina, a "Beautifully Restored Historic Town" of "Picturesque Buildings, Gardens, and Landscape," Founded in 1766 by Moravians, Where You Can Experience "Early American History" and Learn about "Historic Methods and Practices That Remain Relevant Today"

The Music of the Land

When the Moravian brethren first arrived,
staying in an abandoned cabin,
they composed a hymn of Thanksgiving,
"singing it to the accompaniment of wolves."
The books and histories emphasize the music:
how someone made a trumpet from a branch,
and the men sang as they cut down trees;
how the Indians didn't attack Bethabara,
apparently put off by the strange musical sounds;
and how "there isn't a breath of air in Salem
that hasn't been blown through a horn, at least once,"

and when we arrived, staying, as well,
in a house already built,
we too raised our voices,
singing new music,
and sometimes we made instruments
from the materials we found,
the son, especially, adept at turning
anything at hand into percussion,
the world, itself, to him a drum.

What wolves and natives have been kept at bay
by the banging and strange sounds inside our walls?
Or by our disconcerting answers
to the constant *Where do you go to church?*
Because on Sundays, we go to the Church
of Lowe's, this old house needing
repair, renovation and reconstruction.
And sometimes as we pound and mulch,
we hear church bells from Old Salem,
and some years, on Easter morning,
when a band plays at God's Acre at dawn,
trumpeting the news—The Lord has risen!—
we wake up, imagining we have heard it.

Questions

On the Interstate, my daughter tells me
she only has two questions. I'm relieved
because she usually has two hundred.
I say, *Okay, let's have them*, and she asks,
What was there before there was anything?
Stupidly, I think I can answer this:
There was grass, forests, fields, meadows, rivers.
She stops me. *No, Daddy. I mean before
there was anything at all, what was there?*
I say that I don't know, so then she asks,
Where do we go when we die? I tell her
I don't know the answer to this either.
She looks out the side, and I look forward,
then she asks if we can have some music.

Singing in God's Acre

The Moravian choir system is designed to keep you with like-minded people.
—Old Salem Tour Guide

In God's Acre, people are buried chronologically,
in the order they died, rather than next to family,
everyone getting a similar stone and space.
No matter their status in life, here they are equal,
with uniform white markers aligned in rows,
like spread out pages from the same book,
and each contains the same information: name,
dates, a phrase from a hymn or scripture.

The Lord Is My Strength and My Salvation

    Jesus Makes My Heart Rejoice

The stones are repetitive, the same sentiments
again and again, the harmony of the collective,
no solos, even in death singing together,
especially in death, singing together.

But listen and the repetitive insistence
itself begins to suggest a dissonance.

He is not dead. Only sleeping.

All is well.
    All is well.
        All is well.

We Knew Him. We Loved Him. We Miss Him.

    She is not dead.

as if the markers are tablets for others
to write upon and convince themselves.
And the stones with *Loving Husband* and *Mother,*
or images—a Masonic symbol, a crying lamb—
show an unwillingness to erase certain identities.

Listen and you can hear a lingering attachment
to the relationships of this world, a yearning
for those from whom they've been segregated,
a reminder of the price for singing in the choir.

Death and My Daughter: A Timeline

When she is three,
we drive back roads,
and each time she sees
a cemetery, she yells
with delight, *Look!*
More dead people!

When she is four,
as we come home
from daycare, she says,
Daddy, when I'm dead,
please don't leave me outside
in the rain to get wet.
Please bring me inside. Please.

At five, she tells her grandmother,
I know what happens when you die.
You either get boxed up or cooked.

At six, she assures me
as I work on the roof,
Don't worry, Daddy, I'm here.
If you fall and break your legs,
I'll go get Maman. If you fall
and die, I'll call 9-1-1-1-1.
Don't worry, I'm right here.

And when the neighbor dies
and her kindergarten classmate dies,
and her friend's baby brother dies,
what upsets her is the silence
that follows. After the memorials
no one mentions them anymore.
It's like they've just disappeared.
So, at seven, she says, *Please,*
please talk about me after I'm dead,
and when we admit we hope

to die first, she gets worried.
But, I'd be lonely without you.
Maybe we can all die together, she says,
and that way we can stay together.
I want us to stay together, she says,
but we'll need a pretty big box.

Passivity

Because owning made more sense
than renting, the Moravians debated
whether to buy Johann Samuel,
the fifteen-year-old boy
they were leasing from a farmer
to work in their stockyards.
Then they did as they did
with most difficult decisions,
leaving it up to God by casting lots.
They put in three slips of paper—
Yes, No, and a blank one
(which would mean nothing
should be decided then) —
and they pulled one out.
Thus, in 1765, as the brethren
established a communal society
based on a "unity of brotherhood,"
they asked whether the church,
which had come to the area,
in part, to escape persecution,
should become a slave holder.

"The answer came in the affirmative."

Bound

I'm delighted my daughter
feels free to be a tom boy,
climbing trees, tumbling,
running and racing around
with the neighborhood kids,
and I feel like Andy Griffith
or Mike Brady, as I watch
the children go from playing
duck duck goose and tag
to cowboys and ninjas,

and then one afternoon,
one sunny summer afternoon,
the air as sweet as lemonade,
I see the sons of my friends,
pulling my tied-up daughter
along the sidewalk with rope,
two white blond boys
dragging my black daughter
towards a tree. All three
are laughing. It's a game.
A fun game.
                                With rope.

Stop! I yell, unable to keep
the anger and fear and horror
from my voice. The children
look towards me, puzzled,
heads cocked like dogs
at an unexpected sound.

You need to stop because

because

                    because

it's almost time for lunch.
Go and wash your hands.
Everyone wash your hands.

Fragments of Education

One brochure explains how
some Moravian immigrants
learned English and the skills
needed to survive and flourish
from black craftspeople.

Another says how some began
to absorb the "segregationist sentiment
spreading across the new republic."

The tour guide mentions
how some protested the decision
that allowed the church to have slaves,
and they petitioned and were granted
the right to individual ownership,

and the three school girls ask
what time the gift shop closes.

Branded

On the way to the grocery, my daughter asks,
Daddy, Does it hurt to be branded?
Since we had been talking about lemonade
and whether the pink kind tastes different
than the yellow, the question surprises me.
Of course, I say, and she wants to know
how I know and how it's done and why
someone would do it to someone else.
She's been reading the novel *Chains*,
whose heroine gets branded on the cheek,
so as we pass Borders, Pier 1 Imports,
and World Market, we talk about scars,
hot metal, the small crescent burned
into her calf by a car's exhaust pipe.
We talk about how branding compares
with tattooing, why people would do either,
and the difference between being forced
and choosing to do something. We talk
about what you carry on your body
for life, and what kind of a tattoo
we would get, whether we'd have a word
or an image. We talk about how words
from a story or a book or a classmate
can sear and disfigure. We talk about if
what you get on your body is different
than what you get on your tombstone.
She asks what can be written on bones,
and we talk about archaeology and graves,
and then suddenly she says she thinks
pink probably doesn't taste different,
but the eye makes you think that it does.

My Daughter Continues to Be Annoyed by George Washington

A plaque on the Salem Tavern says,
"George Washington slept here."
It's true, it's well documented,
and it doesn't impress my daughter.
She's not a fan. She hasn't been
since she was six and learned
how Washington freed his slaves
on his deathbed. *He waited,*
she said, *until he didn't need them,*
and they were probably too old
to enjoy their freedom then.
Later, looking at her allowance,
she insisted, *George Washington*
shouldn't even be on the dollar.
When I offered to keep the money,
I saw the struggle, the realization
this wasn't how it should be,
but how it is. These symbols
are the ones we live with.
No, she said, *I'll take it,*
sensing as she did so
that she had been forced
to participate in something
under the guise of choice.
Now, at the Salem Tavern
where the first President walked,
she reads the sign out loud,
"George Washington slept here,"
and asks, *"Where did his slaves sleep?"*

Market

At the upscale Farmer's Market,
the one between Salem Tavern
and the landscaped gardens,
I have to put my son in time out.

He sits on the cobblestones crying,
and a church-dressed woman
steps between us and asks him,
"Are you lost? What's wrong?"

Although I'm tempted to see
what he'll do, I say, "He's fine.
He's in time-out." She turns
and sees a stern white man

standing with his arms crossed
(metaphorically if not literally),
a stereotypical figure of authority.
"Why?" she asks, and I know

what she means, but I say,
"Because I put him there."
She works it out, eventually,
but still asks, "Is he yours?"

The familiar question always jars,
the possessive pronoun evoking
other markets, branding, papers
signifying ownership, and also

some people's belief adoption is
buying babies, but saying "yes"
means we all can move along,
so I nod, "I'm his. We're family.

Thank you for being concerned."
Then I tell my son, "You can get up.
Please, stop banging on the booths.
Let's find some flowers for Maman."

For Unknown Reasons

For unknown reasons, in 1913, the few gravestones in this cemetery were pulled up and the churchyard was landscaped...
　　　　—Historical Marker, Old Salem African-American Cemetery, 1815-1859

In 1815, the brethren decided
to segregate the graveyards,
no longer allowing Negroes
to be buried in God's Acre,
no longer considering all
equal after death, no longer
believing in the potential
brotherhood of man.
Right before the Civil War,
the cemetery was closed,
and fifty years later erased,
then, in 1952, Old Salem, Inc.
was chartered, and the church
was relocated miles away
"with the encouragement
of the white church leadership."

Put the dates together,
and you have a timeline
of the pushing away
of blackness, making clear
those "unknown reasons."

Now, you can stand on a hill
overlooking the reconstructed church building,
and what you hear may not be music,
or the voice of the Union chaplain
reading the Emancipation Proclamation
to a congregation of slaves,
or even the line from *Easy Rider*—
"We blew it"—that repeating refrain
of America and its lost opportunities,

what you hear may be the bones
of brothers and sisters,
buried and bulldozed,

but still here,
bones insistently whispering
names and stories and existence
into the dirt,
up through the grass,
and into every breath of air.

Simple Architecture

I tour the African-American church with my son
who would rather be back outside collecting rocks.
The guide points out the architecture is simple
to keep people's mind on God, and I remember
reading how Moravian hymns were composed
so everyone could sing them. I think of how
I'm searching for the right forms for these poems,
ones as simple and solid as wooden bowls,
then my son tugs my hand and asks, "Daddy,
do you like church?" I try not to lie to my kids,
so I say, "No. Not really," and he says, "Good,"
thinking this means we'll be done soon.
The guide explains changes to the building
and mentions the "beautification project"
that landscaped over the churchyard graves
a century ago as if it was just a misguided attempt
to make the town a little more picturesque.

After the tour, I look at the wall outside
that lists 181 names that have been separated
from their bodies as my son returns
to gathering rocks. He will give these
to his mother, not thinking to tell her
about the church or cemetery. He'll say,
"I pet a black cat," and "We had donuts."
Later he'll cry when he thinks the stones
have been lost. His mother will assure him
they're in a beautiful bowl on her desk,
and I'll debate whether to tell her how
he found them on the gravesites of children,
ones whose names have been lost
so each marker now says simply "child,"
and this is only known because of the size
of the bones. I will debate whether to write
any of this, afraid of what I'm bulldozing,
afraid of what I'm beautifying, afraid
I don't fully understand the ground

I'm building upon and that I don't know
what is ours and should remain unspoken
and what is ours and must be said.

Landscaping

After the next door neighbor dies,
the house's new owner hires a crew
to fill in the concrete backyard pool
that's been empty for several decades.
Before they do, they throw in pipes,
metal porch furniture, screens, rags,
boxes of mason jars, paint cans, tools,
trash from a shed, then the shed itself,
tires, tiles, azalea bushes she grew
with cuttings from her father's grave,
then they bulldoze the yard level
and roll out sod. All afternoon
my children stand silent at the fence,
watching, fascinated and apprehensive.

Birth Poems

The 1799 birth certificate
has a poem in its design.
We read it, admire the art,
and then my daughter asks,
"Daddy, what's my birth poem?"
I say, "You don't have one,"
and walk to the next display.

She asks, "Have you looked?"
She knows sometimes I leave
for work with the wrong lunch
or wearing mismatched socks.
A thing like this could have gone
right by me. Or it could be
buried in her adoption records.

I tell her that I'm sure,
then I suggest that maybe
her birth poem is hers
to write. I hope that this
will sound inspirational
or, somehow, poetic,
but when I say it out loud,
it just sounds dumb.

What I should have done
is figure out what she wants.
Does she want me to tell her
her life started with a poem?
That she has a heritage
of beauty and verse? That
poets sing of her as well?

"I don't have one either," I say.
She nods and then suggests,
"Maybe we can write each other's."
This makes no sense either,
but I like the sound of it.
I sip my coffee. "Maybe,
that's what we're doing now."

Dixie

Walking home from Old Salem, we hear singing
coming from a small cinder-block building
that's been abandoned for years, but now is
The Ecclesiastes New Faith Deliverance Center.
We stand outside the windows for a moment
and listen to hymns in Spanish. We don't speak
Spanish, so we don't know what they're saying,
and yet we know exactly what they're saying.

How long does it take to be from around here?
When did that Japanese weed, kudzu, become
Southern? When did Moravians, immigrants,
start claiming the land by tradition and heritage?
Was it when they formed marching bands
for the Confederacy? Or when their children
began talking differently than them? Was it
when they considered others as newcomers?

It's doubtful there will ever be a plaque here,
a reconstruction of these lichen-covered bricks
or a historical reenactment of this service,
yet it's the same story as the one being told
and sold at the Old Salem Visitor's Center:
the forming of a community of fellowship,
the singing together in a strange new land,
the rooting and blossoming of belonging.

Here

Where are you from?
my children are asked,
not because of how they talk,
or how they look, but how
we look with one another,
this unfamiliar form of family
we have put together,
and when they answer, *Here,*
North Carolina, the South,
they're not believed.
Africa, a classmate says,
Your parents adopted you
from there.
                    No,
my daughter explains,
I was born in Charlotte.
The girl continues to insist,
No. Somewhere in Africa.

My daughter comes home,
where she's lived all her life,
where she recognizes everyone
on both sides of the street,
where she intimately knows
each tree in a three-block radius,
and she recounts the discussion.
We all agree it's puzzling
and wonder how to respond.
We ask if there's something
she wants us to do. Perhaps
talk to the teacher or parents?
Yes, she says, there is something.
Maybe, before dinner,
we could put on some music,
and dance together, here,
in our house, our family,
such as it is, such as we are.

III.

THE LAST SPEAKERS OF A LANGUAGE

We Were Only Going to Stay a Year or Two

The way my children speak sounds strange to me.
They put unnecessary syllables
in words, and watching football, my son says,
"Daddy, that's just a big ole mess." It's odd
that I can name almost all the children
in the neighborhood, where they go to school,
and the jobs their parents have or have lost.
I nod to strangers. I give directions
according to where places used to be.
I no longer think anything about
taking the neighbors' garbage cans to the curb.
This is how it happens. Roots grow. Or don't.
In the spring, no one should bother asking
dogwoods if they intended to flower.

We've Had This Conversation Before

We've had this conversation before,
my daughter and I, many times,
about what she might buy
with her allowance, about candy,
about how her brother annoys her,
about where her birth mother might be,

and we've had this conversation before,
my son and I, many times,
about how fast he is, how fast horses are,
about candy, about how his sister bosses him,
about how much a horse costs,

and we've had this conversation before,
my wife and I, many times,
about how tired we are,
about what we might buy them
and how much it all costs,
about how they annoy us, how fast
they're growing, how scared we are
about what might happen, about this life,
this life, so tiring and wonderful,
and how, if we could, we'd repeat it,
this life, many times,
many times.

Relativity

It's when they go back to visit favorite teachers,
you realize just how much they've grown.
They were those small kids on the playground
days ago, and even then you kept remarking
how big they were getting and how quickly.
Stop it, you would say, pushing on their heads.
Once you held them in the palm of your hand
and carried them in a pocket; soon, they won't fit
in the car, the house, your life as it's shaped now.

The Girl in the Second-Story Window

She combs her hair as she looks
at the street or maybe at herself
in the reflection, and I suspect
there's a Chinese poem about this
written centuries ago,

                            but no,
she's on a cell phone, not seeing
the dark wet trees, the stranger
who, looking up, for a moment,
thinks of Li Po, then of a girl,
how they would talk on the phone
for hours, desperate for connection,
and who might be a mother now,
even a grandmother, or dead long ago.

What We Haven't Read

We play the party game,
admitting what we haven't read.
Jane Eyre, Madame Bovary,
anything of Faulkner's.
Amid mock gasps, we name titles
with a mix of embarrassment,
swagger, and relief
that we can finally reveal
how we've never made it
more than twenty pages
into *Portrait of a Lady,*
Middlemarch, Moby Dick.
We don't bother pretending
we'll get to them eventually.
We're confessing, but unrepentant,
and then we begin to get serious:
the newspaper, warning labels,
the mortgage, legal contracts,
every Christmas card from her
for the last twenty years,
the letter he sent before he died,
the lab's blood results last month
and this month and next month.

Trespass

The neighbor's old dog totters splay-legged
to the porch's edge and barks as we pass.
He sounds like a three-pack-a-day smoker.
I consider acting scared and running
as a gesture of generosity,
like when my father growls and slams his hand
on the table. You can barely hear it,
but I pretend to pay more attention.
I bet the dog, however, is too sharp
to really think he's chasing me away,
then I recognize my dad is as smart,
and that it's not me either cares about,
but another, the one who refuses
to pass by no matter how much we bark.

Azaleas

The azaleas shimmer purple
against the white shingles
of the neighbor's house,
luminous in the morning air,
and although the dog tries
to pull me along, straining
towards home and breakfast,
I stand and stare.
Later I'll remember how
Parsifal was paralyzed
by blood drops on snow
and how Frost's traveler
stopped in the woods,
but for now, I think
of nothing,

anchored by color
on color,
blood pulsing,
a taut leash,

then, as the planet continues
its rotation,
the light shifts,
and the azaleas fade
becoming again
flowers, just flowers,
and I am turned back
to my life,
to being someone
concerned with what
the neighbors might think
about an unshaven man
motionless outside their house,
to someone with a dog
eager to be fed.

The Question

Why write a poem
about these trees swaying
against a plum-dark sky?
Why write about the wind
scudding clouds and rain inland?

It's not to remember the moment,
to understand or share it.
It's not to bear witness
to the world's strange beauty
or make some statement
about nature or transience.
It's none of those clichés
that sound profound,
and may even be true,
but come later,
like all explanations,
inadequate and calcifying.

Even a skillful description
of these trees and sky
is not our trees and sky,
which are ours
because of the cheap Bordeaux
we've been drinking for hours,
the soreness from walking,
the bread, the sea air, the stones,
the fact we've known each other
so much longer than we thought
we would. We have survived
and now find ourselves here,
silhouetted in this late light,
in these lives that leak poems
like runoff from storm-shook trees.

Savings

Last night we set the clocks back,
gaining an extra hour to sleep
or drink or read, and I walked
through the house changing the time
in the coffee maker, the stove,
the VCR, the thermostat,

then I went into the bathroom
to twist the dial of the scale
a few pounds lighter,
and I moved the numbers down
on the blood pressure machine
so my wife won't need as many pills,

then to the children's rooms,
to erase the doorframe marks
and repencil them slightly lower,
not to the point we again would need
strollers or slings, just an inch or two,
to make these days last longer.

Catch

She's been in the hospital a week,
this time with no improvement,
and I've come home to shower,
change clothes, and feed the dog.
As I'm about to get back in the car,
the boy next door, whose dad left
years ago, asks if I'll play catch,
and I agree because it's something
I can do. We toss a tennis ball
back and forth in the driveway;
after awhile his mother comes out
with two beers and a juicebox.
She watches, without speaking,
because we have known each other
a long time, and, as it gets darker,
the ball seems to become lighter,
floating through the gloaming.
Maybe I should say it looks
meaningful, like a radioisotope
or a pill, but I'm not thinking
anything like that or about how
we probably look like a family
to passersby. I'm not thinking
at all. I'm just swinging my arm,
grabbing and releasing yellow,
slowly becoming indistinct.

It's a Wonderful Life. It's a Wonderful Life. It's a Wonderful Life.

She says she's fine and I believe her
until she says it again, "I'm fine."
Then again, "No, really, I'm fine,"
and I realize, Ohhhh, something
is wrong, just as we understand
the more Antony repeats Brutus is
an honorable man, the clearer it becomes
we shouldn't believe it.

So what to make of the annual showing
of Capra's film, one considered to be
"inspirational" and "heartwarming,"
one in which the beloved Jimmy Stewart
cracks, attacks his wife and children,
and stands inches from suicide,
one that starts to answer what happens
to dreams deferred, but then covers
what it discovers in a soft falling snow?

It's a wonderful life, no really, it is,
we see and hear and say each year,
vaguely realizing something may be
wrong, meaning accumulating
becoming heavy enough to endanger us
and then, wondrously, melting away.

Ascension

You can chart the children's growth over the years
in the rise and spread of ornaments up the tree.
As toddlers, they create a skirt of decorations.
A single branch might have a half dozen bulbs
clinking together. Most are haphazardly secured,
so they periodically fall, bouncing and breaking
on the floor, like a John Cage holiday soundtrack.
As arm spans increase, balls cover more boughs,
and the children begin to have favorite pieces,
ones they make a point of finding a "good place" for.
And then one year, you realize that they understand
the larger whole, that they are striving for balance,
and that they recognize the importance of finding
the dark spaces to try to fill them with color and light.

Santa's Grace

Even before they stop believing,
children sense the fundamental lie.
They will get what they get regardless
of their behavior. There is no relationship
between being naughty or nice
and what's found under the tree.
They know—everyone knows—
each year the bad are rewarded
along with the good.

This may be just as well.
As Hamlet warns Polonius,
"Treat every man after his desert
and who should 'scape whipping?"
But why then the shiny charade?
The insistence on merit and good works?
Is a bounty akin to unfathomable grace
too difficult to explain? Perhaps
indiscriminate generosity seems unfair,
or we're ashamed of the cold truth
that Santa spends more at different houses.

Wrap up the holiday in any trappings you like;
what happens is inexplicable.
Even children sense it.
And this may be its very appeal.
In a dark season, the world again
seeming to be ending,
we wake to find gifts,
ones that have nothing to do
with what we have done or deserve,
each an invitation to be joyful.
Irrationally joyful.

What We Still Might Have Left

In one of those Christmas specials,
an old magician sits in a stone cell
and inventories the few resources
he has left: a couple of weak spells
and a handful of magic kernels.

I used to think the scene was sad,
this once-powerful wizard coldly
surveying his diminishment, but
now that I'm closer in age to him
than the hero, I see it differently.

As the days grow shorter and darker,
and our powers decline, we might
yet have a trick or two that surprises,
and somewhere loose in our pockets,
among the lint and keys and tissues,

we still may have a few magic seeds,
ones that can grow into something
wondrous, something that can crack
open this frozen ground, these walls,
and even our old ice-crusted hearts.

The End

The end is usually anti-climatic.
No explosions. No fireworks.
No music. Yet it's not a whisper
or whimper either. It happens
as you sort laundry and shop for groceries.
Sometimes you don't even know it is the end
just as the river moves into the delta
dissipating itself before reaching the sea.

The Last Speakers of a Language

My son asks for the cheesehonker.
I don't get it for him right away because
I don't know what it is. He raises his voice
"Cheesehonker!
                    CheeseHonker!"
When I ask, "You want the Cheesehonker?"
he becomes enraged. "No," he yells,
"Cheesehonker!" Finally I say, "Show me,"
and he toddles to his bedroom and points
at the rubble. I rule out anything he can reach,
but nothing else seems like a Cheesehonker,
so I start holding up objects at random.
When I get to a sparkly key ring, he grabs it
and waddles away.

                    That was years ago,
and now only my wife understands
when I ask where the cheesehonker is.
Just as we're the only ones who still talk
of popcheeps and things worth two dotties.
We learned the vocabulary of our children,
and then they grew away from it, leaving us
the last speakers of a language, the curators
of a way of life that briefly flourished, then,
as the door jamb marks rose, disappeared.

Spring Is Icumen In

So spring has come again
again the buds and birds
again the breeze that makes
it seem so much is possible.
Again this miraculous turning
outside and in, the greening
and growth, outside and in,
again this desire to write
a poem, yet another one
about spring, and the heart
hatching in a nest of bones,
the same poem written
last year and the year before,
the one that's been written
each spring for centuries,
this one, again and again.

Thanks are due to the MakeGroup of Bob King, Betsy Towns, and Dean Wilcox for their encouragement, to Kevin Watson for his constant support, to Sean O'Grady for his invaluable critical eye, and, especially, to Danielle Tarmey without whom this material, this life, would not exist.

JRM

A born and bred Northerner, JOSEPH MILLS is now raising two born and bred Southerners, ones who sometimes say things like, "Daddy, I'll cut the lights." He teaches at the University of North Carolina School of the Arts where he holds an endowed chair, the Susan Burress Wall Distinguished Professorship in the Humanities. In addition to five poetry collections, he is the co-author (with his wife Danielle Tarmey) of *A Guide to North Carolina's Wineries.* He also edited *A Century of the Marx Brothers.* Every New Year's Eve he resolves to improve his guitar playing and learn how to cook more interesting dishes; the fact that each year he genuinely believes this will happen reveals a fundamentally optimistic nature.

Cover artist KENNETH FRAZELLE is an accomplished and acclaimed composer who teaches at the University of North Carolina School of the Arts in both the Music School and the School of Filmmaking. His music has been commissioned and performed by Yo-Yo Ma, Jeffrey Kahane, Jan DeGaetani, Gilbert Kalish, and many others. Frazelle first received international acclaim with his score for *Still/ Here*, a multimedia dance theater work for the Bill T.Jones/Arnie Zane Dance Co. Frazelle has received awards and fellowships from the American Academy of Arts and Letters, the American Academy in Rome, and Columbia University, and he was the winner of the 2001 Barlow Prize, the international competition administered through Brigham Young University. He has held residencies with the Los Angeles Chamber Orchestra, the Santa Rosa Symphony, and the Isabella Stewart Gardner Museum. Frazelle was a pupil of Roger Sessions at The Juilliard School and attended high school at the North Carolina School of the Arts, where he studied with Robert Ward.

Also an accomplished painter, of his untitled watercolor, he says, "It's a miniature, postcard-sized painting, a quick depiction of the rounded meadow above our garden in the Blue Ridge Mountains of Virginia. I'm intrigued by the precarious gravity suggested by hilly places. The way the gold and brown pigments dissipate into a corona near the trees was unplanned—one of the 'happy accidents' of the watercolor medium."

Learn more about Kenneth Frazelle's music and paintings at kennethfrazelle.blogspot.com.